This lovely Book belongs to

Name ...............................

Address ...............................

...............................

...............................

# GRAHAM RAWLE

# WONDER BOOK

## OF

# FUN

A Harvest Original
Harcourt Brace & Company
San Diego   New York   London

HARCOURT BRACE & COMPANY
1919–1994
SEVENTY-FIVE YEARS

Acknowledgments

Special thanks to:

Georgia Garrett, Liz Knights, George Sharp,
Margaret Huber, Denis Rawle, Jeff Rawle,
David Hiscock, Ian Craig, the Barsuhns,
Katrina Whone, and all at Gollancz.

First published in Great Britain 1993 by Victor Gollancz
© Graham Rawle 1993

ISBN 0-15-600094-6

First Harvest edition 1994

A B C D E

Printed in Great Britain

For my big brother Jeffrey

# Contents

# A puzzle that will interest you!

A    B    C

# Bomb Sombrero!

Three women are blindfolded and lined up in a row, one behind the other. A man has five hats, three red and two yellow. He puts a hat on each of the women and locks the remaining two hats in a cupboard.

The women are told they can remove their blindfolds, and if they can work out the colour of their own hat they must shout 'Bomb

to turn around or to look at their own hat.

C takes off her blindfold and says nothing. B takes off her blindfold and also remains silent. Without removing her blindfold, A shouts 'Bomb Sombrero!' and correctly states the colour of her hat.

What colour was her hat and how

Poor old Pete has been wrongfully imprisoned
and the only way to free him is to remove the scissors
without cutting or untying the cord.
Can you help, for Pete's sake?

## HALFWAY UP THE LADDER

This man is on his way home but he has bought so many things at the market that he is unable to climb the ladder carrying them all.

Halfway up the ladder is a boy who might help him but the boy says, "I will help you only if you can correctly predict whether or not I will help you."

The man says, "You will not help me." Does the boy help him or not?

**H**ow can these six pieces be assembled to form a letter H?

# THIEF IN THE NIGHT

**1** When the famous Bellingham jewels are reported stolen, Police Headquarters are at once notified. When Inspector Armstrong arrives at the scene, Nurse Evelyn – a resident at the Bellingham household – explains her story.

**2** 'I was just home from a party and had taken off my dress as it was rather hot. I decided to listen to the radio before going to bed. Sitting in my underwear I soon noticed a draught from the open window. I distinctly remembered having closed and locked the window before going out.'

**3** I suspected something was wrong and my suspicions were confirmed when I saw that a ladder had been placed at the open window. Someone must have climbed the ladder and forced the latch.

**4** I quickly ran to Lady Bellingham's jewellery box to see if anything was missing and found the box completely empty. The thief had taken the famous Bellingham jewels.

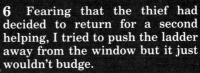

**6** Fearing that the thief had decided to return for a second helping, I tried to push the ladder away from the window but it just wouldn't budge.

**5** I was about to dial 999 when I heard a noise at the open window. Keeping out of sight I tried to see who was there but it was too dark.

**7** It was then that Constable Pugh appeared at the window. He'd seen the ladder from the street and had climbed up to investigate.

**8** He quickly summoned you, Inspector Armstrong, and here we both are.'
'You're lying!' snaps Armstrong.

HOW DID HE KNOW?

# PRODUCING RIBBON FROM A TANGERINE

◆

**YES, BUT HOW IS IT DONE?**

**T**HREAD a piece of narrow ribbon about twelve inches long on to a large needle until about half an inch is protruding from the eye. Now twist the tail of the ribbon tightly round the needle towards the point.

Holding the point, press a small tangerine on to the head of the needle until the eye appears at the other side. Now unthread the protruding half-inch of ribbon and remove the needle, leaving the twisted thread hidden inside the tangerine.

Children and adults alike will be amazed. Imagine how loudly they will shout "Hoorah!" as you commence to pull ribbon from a tangerine.

# THE ROAD TO RUINATION

A man is pushing a car towards a hotel. When he reaches the hotel he will become bankrupt. Why?

This picture may give you a clue but it will not furnish you with the answer.

## MR. MYERS READS YOUR MIND

Think of a number between 1 and 10 (but not 1 or 10) and multiply it by 9. Add together the two digits of your answer and subtract 5. Now if A=1, B=2, C=3 and so on, then find the letter that corresponds to the number you are left with, and think of a country that begins with that letter. Now think of a four-legged animal whose name begins with the *second* letter of that country. Got one? Good.

Now turn to page 59 to see if Mr. Myers can read your mind.

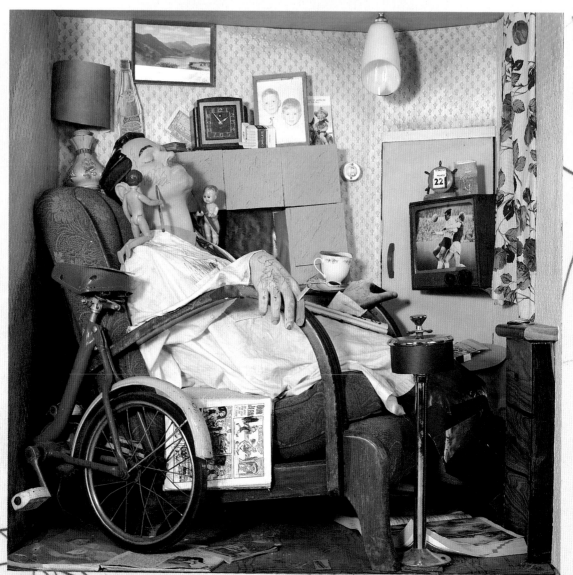

**I**T is Wednesday, half-day closing, and having shut the shop Uncle Stan settles down for his afternoon nap. Every week on this day his two nephews, Jeffrey and Graham, come to stay and while he is asleep he lets them each take a pen from his pocket and scribble all over his hands. On special occasions, like today, they are allowed to scribble on his face as well.

Each has a ball-point pen which when full can draw a line one mile long. Jeffrey's pen is half full and Graham's pen is three-quarters full. Jeffrey draws at the rate of one yard in six seconds. Graham, being younger, takes nine seconds. However, Jeffrey's pen is faulty and every fifty yards it goes dry and it takes him one minute to get it going again.

Uncle Stan has the television on for the football, and as the kick-off whistle blows for the match to begin Uncle Stan dozes off and the boys start scribbling.

After the customary ninety minutes, plus fifteen minutes' half-time, Stan hears the final whistle and wakes up, with his face covered in ink, to discover that he has missed the entire match.

At the time of his waking, which nephew's pen is still working and who has been responsible for most of the ink on Uncle Stan's face?

Lebrun, Leblanc and Lenoir are triplets born on the same day, yet on the day before yesterday Lebrun was forty years old and next year Leblanc will be forty-three.

·❖·

How old is Lenoir?

# EVEN A DOG HAS A LOVELY PIE

This doggie has a lovely pie waiting for him at home but he can't for the life of him remember which path takes him there. Can you help?

# *Time waits for Norman*

NORMAN woke to find everything in his room exactly as he had left it. Nothing had moved during the night – the furniture, the fireplace and his trousers were all where they should have been – yet Norman knew at once that something was missing.

It was unusually quiet and it soon dawned on him that the clock on his wall was no longer ticking. He had forgotten to wind it and during the night it had stopped. This presented a problem for Norman as the clock was his only time-piece and he had no other way of knowing the correct time.

He had arranged to visit his uncle that morning, who was in hospital recovering from a hip replacement operation. It was a sunny day so rather than take the bus Norman decided to walk.

At the hospital there was a clock that was working and showed the correct time. Norman went and sat with his uncle for a while, chatting, playing draughts and listening to the radio. When visiting time was over, Norman walked home again.

Since he didn't know the exact length of his journey, how was Norman able to set his clock correctly on his return?

# SOME WONDERFUL SHEEP

**THE WALLACHIAN SHEEP**

This wild sheep is a horned animal. Over the centuries horns have disappeared in some breeds and multiplied in others. Here the horns have become twisted like a corkscrew. The Wallachian is found in such remote regions of the world as Africa and the Hebrides.

**THE AUSIMI SHEEP**

This South African species is required to withstand long periods of scanty pasturage. The fat tail serves as a food reserve for the sheep. The tail often becomes so large and heavy that a trolley is built to support it so the sheep can walk about.

**THE MANED SHEEP OF THE CAMEROONS**

This breed seems to have derived its remarkable colouring from the wild moufflon. It is the smallest breed of sheep in existence. An adult ram stands only nineteen inches at the withers making it ideal for smuggling on to aeroplanes.

**THE UDURU SHEEP**

The double coat of the Uduru, a native of Peru, gives good wool and marketable lambs. In hot weather it grazes mainly at night, storing food in a goitre-like pouch in its neck until morning.

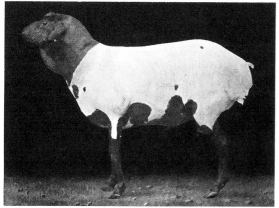

**THE FAT-RUMPED SHEEP**

In central Asia both a black and a white strain are kept, the lambs of the former yielding the famous 'astrakhan' fur. This strange-looking sheep is usually piebald and stores fat in its ample buttocks.

How many of these wonderful sheep
do you think really exist?
Which, if any, have been invented
for your amusement

# VEXED QUESTION
## ? *baffles the professor*

How can Professor Chipchase place eight white balls on a chess board so that no two balls share the same row, column or diagonal?

## TWENTY-FOUR BIRTHDAYS

If twenty-four people were chosen at random, what would you estimate the probability to be that two or more of them would share the same birthday? (Ignore leap years and assume births are evenly spread throughout the year.)

# MYSTERY VOICE

HERE'S a good one. Invite a friend to choose any letter from the alphabet and tell him that the mystery voice will be able to guess the letter he has picked. Once he's made his choice, which he announces to everyone in the room, you dial the secret number and pass the telephone receiver to your friend, who is struck speechless when he hears the voice at the other end tell him the letter he has chosen. How is it done?

**W**hen the ends of these ropes are pulled, some tangles will form a knot.

Can you work out which knots will knot, and which knots will not?

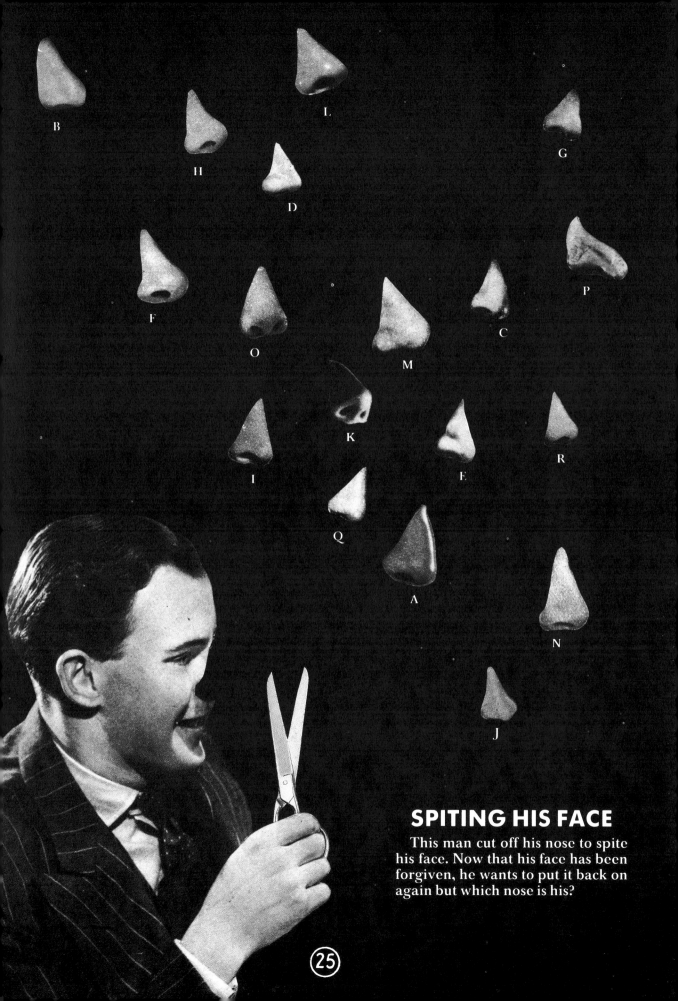

## SPITING HIS FACE

This man cut off his nose to spite his face. Now that his face has been forgiven, he wants to put it back on again but which nose is his?

# THOUGHTS ON COMBING

    I usually like to get an early start. Most days I'm out in the garden combing my hair by a quarter to eight, even earlier in the summer. I don't do much combing inside the house; it isn't the same. As a rule I try not to comb during the night, but I occasionally go out into the garden for half an hour.

I use nylon combs – they're the best. The tortoise-shell variety may look OK but they don't stand up to rigorous use and quite often the teeth snap off. The comb then draws an uneven path through the hair, which becomes impossible to correct.

Sometimes my favourite red comb won't do. After a while it loses its 'combingness' and I have to stop and go inside to fetch another. I have lots of combs indoors.

Once, when I was out in the garden, the wind blew the back door shut. I wanted to swap combs but I couldn't get inside so I had to continue combing with my red comb, even though I would have liked to change it.

Since then I have kept a supply of combs hidden in the garden, though I sometimes worry that I won't be able to find them all.

Can you help me?

# Hat Check TRAGEDY

**A**LL THESE PEOPLE left their hats with the hat check girl, but while they were away a passing lorry shook the building so vigorously that all the hats fell off their hooks and landed in a heap on the floor. When the people returned, the hat check girl accidentally gave each of them the wrong hat.

By studying their outfits carefully, can you see which hat each person should be wearing?

## TEN DESPERADOS

Sheriff Steve, having captured the notorious McBride gang from Painted Canyon, is faced with a problem. He has nine cells in his jail but there are ten men in the gang, and the law says that no two outlaws may share a cell.

To solve this problem, Sheriff Steve takes the first two men and puts them in the cell marked A. The third varmint is assigned to B, the fourth to C and the fifth to D. The sixth baddy goes in cell E, the seventh in F, the eighth and ninth in G and H. He then returns to cell A, where he originally put two of the gang, and taking one of them puts him in cell I.

Sheriff Steve is very pleased with himself for having found a cell for each desperado. Should he be?

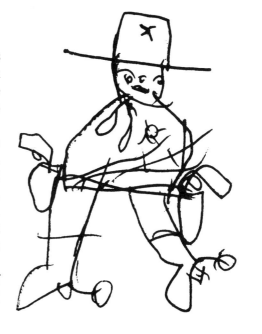

Can you place six cigarettes so that each one touches the other five? Once you've found a solution, try the same thing with seven.

In this picture there are fourteen soldiers, fighting fit and ready for action. Count them for yourself and see. Part of each soldier falls inside the circle, and part outside.

But when the inner circle is rotated so that the red lines match up, only thirteen soldiers remain. The soldiers have swapped halves but now one of them is missing. Which soldier has gone A.W.O.L., and where does he go?

# BALL CONTROL

These two pictures may look the same, but if you study them carefully you should be able to spot ten differences between them.

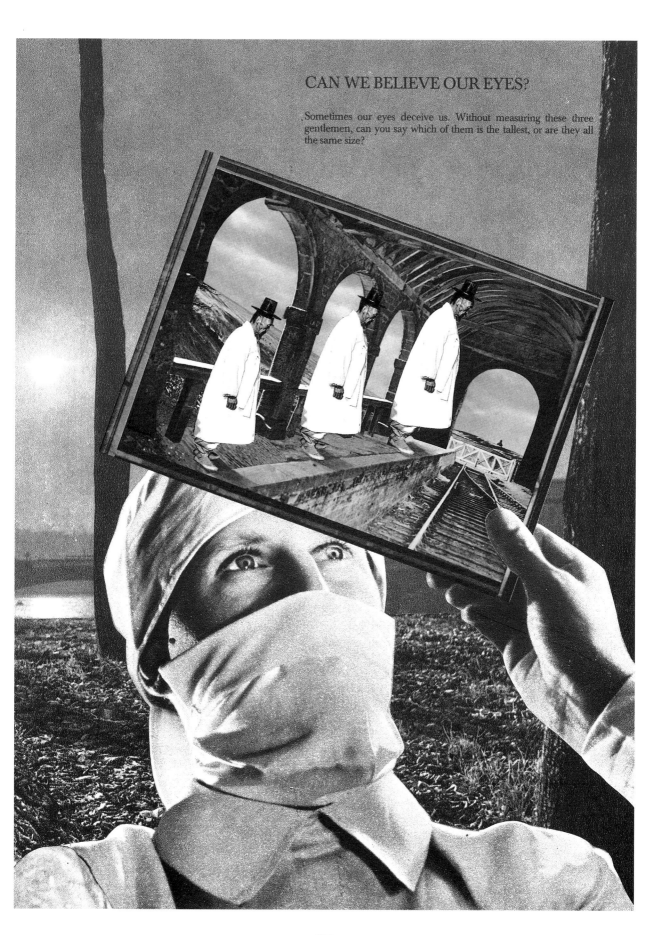

## CAN WE BELIEVE OUR EYES?

Sometimes our eyes deceive us. Without measuring these three gentlemen, can you say which of them is the tallest, or are they all the same size?

**W**illiam Nester had been unhappy at his work for some time. He had grown to hate his job and he could see no way out. One day, as he stood looking through the window on the thirteenth floor of the office building where he worked, he suddenly decided he could stand it no longer. He opened the window and leapt through. It was a sheer drop outside the building to the pavement below. There was nothing to break his fall, yet he did not die, nor did he injure himself in any way. Can you fathom how this could be so?

# Afternoon Tease

**S**IMPSON likes to do things right. Every day he has his afternoon tea at exactly 4 o'clock, and to make absolutely certain that it *is* 4 o'clock he has two watches and he won't begin his tea unless both watches show 4 o'clock precisely.

But what Simpson doesn't realise is that during the night something peculiar has happened and now one of his watches gains a minute in every hour, while the other loses two minutes an hour.

If he sets both watches correctly at noon how long will he have to wait until they both say 4 o'clock and Simpson can begin his tea?

# THE FAMILY WITH FOUR RED FACES

A family of four are told to close their eyes while a man comes into the room and paints each of their faces either red or green. They are told that when they open their eyes if they see a red face they must stand on their chair. If they can correctly state the colour of their own face they must stand on the table.

All four faces were painted red though none of them could see their own face. When they opened their eyes they all stood on their chairs. After a few minutes Mother climbed on to the table.

How did she know her face was red?

Down Boy!
But the naughty dog disobeys his master,
jumping up to bite the Indian Chief.
If they gave him a bone…
But alas there is none;
Or there might be just one
Hidden somewhere in the picture.

# Sneezing Power

A man is sitting on a chair in the centre of a room 20 feet square, the floor surface of which is completely frictionless. The man and his chair together weigh 150lb. Suddenly the man sneezes, expelling half an ounce of nose debris at 100 miles an hour, causing his chair to move backwards. When will the chair reach the wall?

a) in 5 seconds    b) in 55 seconds    c) in 5.5 minutes    d) never

# A MOTHER'S HELPING HAND

When I'm in the garden playing cowboys, Mother tells me to go in the drain outside instead of traipsing all the way upstairs. But no matter how full your water pistol is, if the end is blocked, then nothing will come out.

Next door but one, Mr. Faulkner's wife is driving the family car, a Volkswagen, off the roof of their garage. As the car starts to fall, I can see her face quite clearly through the windscreen. It is a terrible picture but Mother covers my eyes.

The Faulkners are kind to us, so if Mrs. Faulkner *has* died then she will go to heaven. Mr. Faulkner will have to take her there in their other car. It goes at a hundred and fifteen miles an hour. If they set off now, will Mrs. Faulkner be in heaven by the time I get back from hospital, this time next year?

Heaven is a million miles away.

# 3-Way Split

Can you cut this shape into three pieces, using only two straight cuts, so that the pieces can be rearranged to form a square?

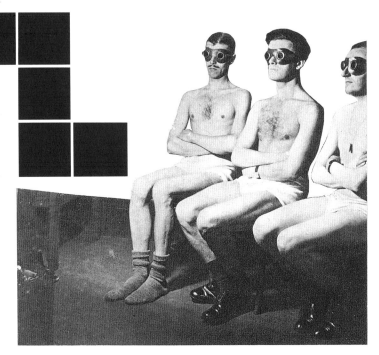

## DEAD MAN'S SHOES

You have inherited a number of shoes from a distant relative, but can you find two that will make a pair?

**I**T'S the night before Christmas and Santa Claus has brought presents for the children who live here. But instead of putting the presents in the children's stockings or leaving them under the Christmas tree, as is customary, Santa has hidden around the room a rifle; a crocodile; a pipe; a motorbike; a fish; a pencil; a cowboy; a screwdriver and a canoe.

Can you find them all?

**C**ount the things in this jolly picture that begin with the letter C. There are over fifty of them in all. How many can you see?

# DISPLACEMENT ACTIVITY

## Can you answer this key question?

A toy boat is floating in a swimming pool. A balloonist passing overhead accidentally drops the key to his mother's house. Which will raise the water level higher, the key landing in the boat or the key landing in the water?

# DOG TOOTH CHECK

a

b

c

d

e

f

g

h

i

Each of these naughty dogs has been caught wearing its owner's teeth.

# A CANINE RIDDLE

By carrying out a thorough check, can you match each dog with its owner?

J UST to see how very wide your eyes are open, I have made several mistakes in this
picture. Make a list of all the errors you can find and turn to the back of the book to
see if you have spotted them all.

# Chomsky's Dream

Chomsky has a cat called Mimi who sleeps at the bottom of his bed at night. When Chomsky is asleep, everything in his dreams that he believes to be true is in fact false. In dreams he believes that chairs can talk and that books can swim. When he's awake he knows that chairs can't talk and that books can't swim because everything Chomsky believes when he's awake is true. One night as the clock strikes midnight, Chomsky believes that both he and Mimi are asleep. Was Mimi in fact awake or asleep?

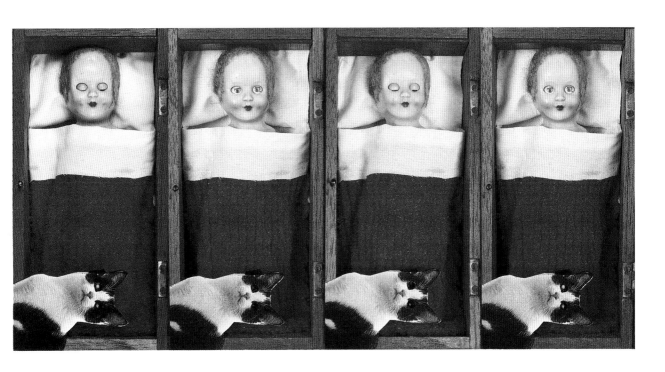

# BALL IN THE MOUTH EFFECT

Float an India rubber ball, about $1^1/_2$ inches in diameter, in a bowl of water and challenge your friends to remove it using only the mouth. This should result in much hilarity and many a wet face.

When your friends have stopped laughing, you can show them how it is done.

The secret is to put your pursed lips close to the ball and then sharply draw in a long breath. Without breathing out, raise your head away from the bowl. Hey presto! The ball is in the mouth.

TRY IT. IT'S GOOD.

# It's your birthday. Hooray! And each of these thoughtful people has baked you a cake. Which cake should you eat?

## Many HAPPY Returns!

**A**

Rhonda Belle Martin worked as a waitress in Montgomery, Alabama. In 1970, doctors, puzzled by her husband Ronald's mysterious illness, carried out extensive tests which revealed the cause to be arsenic poisoning. Ronald's father Claude had died in 1951 displaying symptoms similar to those of his son. When Claude's body was exhumed and found to contain arsenic, police became suspicious of a number of other deaths. Her mother and five of her children had all died unexpectedly. When confronted, she confessed that she had murdered them all with ant poison which she bought at the local grocery store. Enjoy your cake!

**B**

Herbert Armstrong was a small-town solicitor and retired British Army Major living in Hay-on-Wye. In 1921 he found himself in dispute over a professional matter with a rival solicitor, Oswald Martin. Aiming to settle the disagreement, Armstrong invited Martin to his house for tea. He'd prepared some scones especially and offered one to Martin with the words *Excuse fingers*. The scone was poisoned and on returning home Martin was violently ill. Armstrong extended further invitations but Martin refused them all. Armstrong responded by sending Mr & Mrs Martin a box of chocolates that had been injected with arsenic. Enjoy your cake!

**C**

Schoolboy toxicologist *extraordinaire*, Graham Young was arrested aged fourteen charged with poisoning his sister, his father and a school friend. His step-mother had mysteriously died some months previously. Graham's preoccupation continued in Broadmoor. He put sugar soap in the communal tea-urn and piped gas into the night-time cocoa. Ironically, on his release in 1972 he was sent to work at a photo lab in St Alban's where he found endless supplies of his favourite poison, thallium, which he administered to his workmates in welcoming cups of tea. Enjoy your cake!

**D**

Mrs Beeton has been the guide, philosopher and friend of countless happy homes for well over a century. Her *Book of Household Management*, mainly devoted to cookery, was first published in 1861 and has since run into many editions. Mrs Beeton's recipes have rescued generations of young housekeepers from perplexity and domestic woe. Sir Arthur Conan Doyle, who was particularly fond of her delicious date and walnut cake, proclaimed her 'the greatest housekeeper in the world', adding that 'as a cook she is second to none. Therefore Mr Beeton must be the happiest and most comfortable of men'. Enjoy your cake!

**E**

Having successfully nursed Ernest Koch into his grave, and collected a sizable legacy, Anna Hahn decided to make a career out of catering to ill and elderly people. She had already hospitalised her husband by putting him on a diet of poisoned beer and spinach, and quickly achieved an impressive mortality rate amongst her many patients. In 1937, Hahn was convicted of murder and sentenced to the electric chair. During her trial it was revealed that from 1931 to 1937, Anna's 'nursing' had gained her over $70,000. She once avoided repaying an $80 loan from an elderly patient by routinely feeding her ice-cream laced with arsenic. Enjoy your cake!

# Piebald Spotting

There was once a farmer who had two black and white horses called Neddy and Norton. Neddy and Norton were twins and were identical in every way.

The farmer was never kind to his horses and never rewarded them properly for their hard work. Being not only twin brothers but also the best of friends, Neddy and Norton never protested at being worked so cruelly as long as they could be together.

One day, while Neddy and Norton were ploughing the big field, the farmer went out to the woods with his gun, hoping to shoot a rabbit for his supper. When one came into view, he took aim and fired. Bang! The bullet whistled past the rabbit, who scampered away, and sped on to hit Neddy, who was working in the field nearby. The horse fell to the ground, dead.

Norton, who was asleep, witnessed none of this. When the farmer saw what he had done, he was at once concerned. But not for poor Neddy. The farmer's only fear was that without his brother by his side Norton would be filled with such sadness that he would no longer be inspired to work so hard in the fields.

While Norton continued to sleep, the farmer, having hit upon an idea, hurried down to the village, where he bought a large mirror. Back in the field he stood the mirror next to the sleeping horse and buried poor Neddy's body in the woods.

When Norton awoke from his nap he saw his own reflection in the mirror and, assuming it was his twin brother, leapt to his feet ready to start work again. "Come, Brother," he said. "Let us show the old man how hard we can work." And with that he picked up the plough and, head down, set off to work, confident and happy that his brother was beside him.

At the end of the day the whole field was ploughed and Norton, having unwittingly done the work of two, collapsed exhausted beside the mirror. Turning to his reflection he said, "I can see you are as tired as I am, Brother. We have worked well today. Let us now rest."

That night he died and went to heaven.

The farmer was furious to find that his trick had backfired on him. Instead of two fine horses to do his work, he now had none, and from that day on he was forced to carry the heavy plough himself, the mirror only serving to remind him of what he had done.

Meanwhile, in heaven, Norton was having trouble finding Neddy. Horse heaven is full of black and white horses. Yet while there are many black and white horses who look alike, only twins are identical in every way. Can you bring Neddy and Norton together again?

# TALKING SUSAN AND THE THREE RICH UNCLES

On his first day working as a sales assistant in a toyshop, Tony's very first customers are three rich uncles who want to buy a doll for their niece.

Tony shows them a selection of moderately priced dolls but the men say that only the best will do, and they choose the 'Talking Susan' doll, which costs £30.

Each uncle takes a crisp new ten-pound note from his wallet to pay for it, and when the package is wrapped they tip their hats and leave.

Tony is feeling very pleased at having made his first sale until Mr. Cooper, the manager, arrives and announces that the 'Talking Susan' is now on sale and has been reduced from £30 to £25.

"But I've just sold one to three men at the old price," says Tony.

"Good gracious," says Mr. Cooper. "This will never do. We must not overcharge our customers." And with that he takes five £1 notes from the till and sends Tony off to try and catch up with the men so that their five pounds can be returned to them.

Outside on the street Tony spots the rich uncles climbing into their chauffeur-driven car, but as he approaches Tony realises that five pounds cannot easily be divided between three. He decides to tell them that the 'Talking Susan' has only been reduced to £27, which will enable him to give each man one pound back and keep two pounds for himself. This he does and the three uncles are none the wiser.

But if each man has paid nine pounds for a doll that cost £27, and Tony has kept two pounds for himself, making £29, what has happened to the other pound?

Carefully study the pictures on this page for one minute. Close your eyes and see how many of them you can recall.

1–7 Not very good     8–13 Good     14–17 Very good     18–20 Very good indeed

# ROSS SEEKS IT OUT

Brrring Brrring! The loud jangling of the telephone disturbed Inspector Ross, who was working late at Scotland Yard. As he lifted the receiver, he heard a faint voice at the other end. "Hello. This is Victor Wilson, Romney Lodge . . . I've been robbed . . . a tall thin man with a red beard . . ." The voice broke off and Ross heard a muffled groan.

Ross arrived at Wilson's upstairs flat to find the door locked. Peering through the keyhole, he could see Wilson's body slumped across the bed, his features dimly lit by a flickering candle on his bedside table. A safe in the room was open and empty.

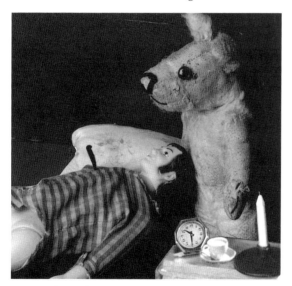

Breaking down the door, Inspector Ross flicked the light switch to find the bulb had blown. Replacing it with a spare from his coat pocket, he switched on the light and extinguished the candle. Wilson – a wealthy recluse – was dead, stabbed in the chest with a letter-opener. He'd died no later than 10 o'clock. All the windows were securely fastened.

Inspector Ross questioned Wilson's landlord, Mark D'Coco, who told him that Wilson had had only one visitor that evening, a tall thin man with a red beard, who had left about half an hour before. Nobody had been in or out since. D'Coco's wife, Ayesha, confirmed this. "Grr!" snapped Ross. "You're lying and you're both under arrest on suspicion of murder."

How did he know?

# 30

**YEARS** ago this man hid seven toys in the forest.
Now, each night in his dreams, he returns to look for them.
The toys lie easily within his reach but the light from his torch can never quite find their hiding places.

Can you help him?

**TOYS TO FIND:** a rhinoceros a horse a car an Indian a whistle a dinosaur a shovel

# SOLUTIONS

*page 8*

## SPLIT PERSONALITIES

*page 9*

## BOMB SOMBRERO!

If C had seen two yellow hats she would have known that her own hat was red. Since she remains silent, she must have seen either two red hats or a red and a yellow. If B had seen a yellow hat she'd have to assume that her own hat couldn't be yellow, otherwise C would have shouted "Bomb Sombrero!"

Since B remains silent, A knows that B cannot have seen a yellow hat, and concludes that her own must be red.

*page 10*

## FOR PETE'S SAKE

Pull on the end of the loop knotted around the left handle. As this loop lengthens, thread it through the scissors following the path taken by the rest of the double cord. When you have passed a sufficient length through the right handle to form a large enough loop, slip the scissors through it, taking care not to twist the cord. When pulled, the scissors will then come away from the cord.

*page 11*

## HALFWAY UP THE LADDER

If the boy had intended not to help him, then the man's prediction would be correct, forcing the boy to help. If the boy *had* intended to help the man, the man's prediction would be wrong so the boy would not help him. But if the boy doesn't help him, then the man's prediction was in fact correct, and if he is correct then the boy must help him.

*page 11*

## PIECES OF AITCH

*page 12*

## THIEF IN THE NIGHT

The ladder projects above the sill of the casement window ledge, which opens outwards. Therefore the ladder must have been placed there *after* the window had been opened, a fact that indicated that Nurse Evelyn was an accomplice of the thief.

Her shameless attempts to distract the inspector, by painting a picture of events in which she wore only her underwear, failed. When confronted with the obvious flaw in her evidence, she confessed.

*page 15*

## ROAD TO RUINATION

The man is playing Monopoly.

*page 15*

## MR. MYERS

Mr. Myers says, "Was it an elephant from Denmark?"

*page 16*

## UNCLE STAN

At exactly the time Uncle Stan wakes up, Jeffrey's pen stops working. Graham is still going strong but his brother has done more scribbling.

Jeffrey's maximum output is 880 yards. At 6 seconds a yard it takes him 6 minutes to scribble 50 yards (5 minutes drawing and 1 minute dry). 880 yards = (50 x 17) + 30 yards, so the time it takes for his pen to empty is (17 x 6) + 3 minutes = *105 minutes*. (He takes only 3 minutes to draw the last 30 yards.)

At 9 seconds a yard, Graham takes 7½ minutes to draw 50 yards. After 105 minutes, when Uncle Stan wakes up, Graham has produced only 700 yards of scribble but still has half his ink left. If Uncle Stan had slept through *Wagon Train* as well, Graham would have drawn the most.

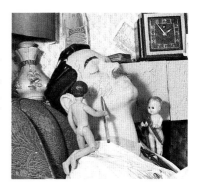

*page 18*

LEBRUN, LEBLANC AND LENOIR

Lenoir is forty-one. His brothers are the same age because they were all born on the same day. The statement was made on January 1st. Their birthday is on December 31st. They were forty the day before yesterday and forty-one yesterday. They will be forty-two at the end of this year, and forty-three next year.

*page 20*

TIME WAITS FOR NORMAN

Before he set off to visit his uncle, Norman wound his clock and set it to a particular time. (Eleven o'clock as it happens.)

He noted the exact time when he arrived at and departed from the hospital, and having walked at the same pace on both journeys noted the time on his clock when he got home.

The elapsed time on his clock is the duration of two journeys plus the time he spent at the hospital.

Since Norman knows the length of time he spent with his uncle, he subtracts this from the elapsed time on his clock and divides the remaining time by two in order to calculate the duration of his journey one way. He then simply adds the journey time to the time he left the hospital, which gives him the correct time.

*page 21*

SOME WONDERFUL SHEEP

Only one of the wonderful sheep is invented. This is the Uduru, which was made from a kangaroo on a goat's body with bicycle handlebars sticking out of its head.

*page 22*

VEXED QUESTION

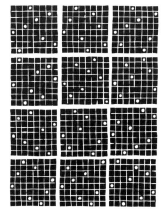

*page 23*

TWENTY-FOUR BIRTHDAYS

It is actually more likely than not that two people will share the same birthday.

The probability that the birthdays of any two people do *not* fall on the same day is clearly 364/365, since there is only a one in 365 chance that one person's birthday will coincide with another's. The probability that a third person's birthday will differ from the other two is 363/365; a fourth person's 362/365, and so on until the twenty-fourth person where the probability is 342/365.

To calculate the probability that all twenty-four birthdays are different, these twenty-three fractions must be multiplied together, and this gives us a fraction which reduces to 23/50, a greater than 50 per cent chance that two people will share the same birthday.

These results are so startling that actually putting them to the test makes for an interesting diversion. Next time you're at a football match, try looking up the birthday of each player in your programme (including one substitute per team). There will probably be two players with the same birthday, and you can point out this interesting coincidence to someone standing next to you.

*page 23*

MYSTERY VOICE

What your friend doesn't know is that you have prearranged this stunt with someone who has agreed to be the mystery voice. When you dial his number and he answers, you say, "Hello, is that the mystery voice?" which is the signal for him to start reciting the alphabet. When he reaches the letter your friend has chosen, you simply stop him by saying, "Hold the line," so that when you pass the receiver to your friend the 'mystery voice' can correctly state the letter he chose.

This trick is particularly effective if the mystery voice hangs up immediately after announcing the letter.

*page 24*

WHICH KNOTS WILL KNOT?

B and C will knot but A will not.

*page 25*

SPITING HIS FACE

Answer: Nose D

*page 26*

THOUGHTS ON COMBING

*page 28*

HAT CHECK TRAGEDY

A–8; B–5; C–7; D–9; E–2; F–1; G–3; H–4; I–6

*page 28*

TEN DESPERADOS

No. The desperado moved from cell A is number two, not number ten.

*page 29*

THE TOUCHING CIGARETTES

*page 32*

BALL CONTROL

*page 33*

CAN WE BELIEVE OUR EYES?

They are not all the same size. Though the man farthest away appears taller because of the perspective in the picture, in fact he *is* slightly taller than the other two.

*page 34*

CRISIS ON THE 13TH FLOOR

William Nester did not die, because he was a window cleaner working on the outside of the building and when he opened the window to jump through it he jumped *into* the building, not out. As a vertigo sufferer, William was clearly in the wrong job. His decision to change careers led to a position in the company's accounts department on the ground floor, where he has been happily employed ever since.

*page 35*

AFTERNOON TEASE

When both watches show 4 o'clock and Simpson begins his tea, it is actually 12 o'clock noon on the eleventh day.

*page 36*

FOUR RED FACES

Mother sees three red faces and stands on her chair. She then thinks "suppose my face is green". If this were the case then Father would see two red faces and one green. If he then thought "suppose *my* face is green", he'd know that his daughter would see one red face (Baby's) and two green.

  If that were the case, the daughter would realise that if her face was green then Baby would not have seen a red face and so would not have stood on his chair. Therefore the daughter knows her face must be red. Father similarly reasons that *his* face is red and Mother, knowing hers is also red, stands on the table.

*page 38*

DOWN BOY!

## page 39

### SNEEZING POWER

The chair will reach the wall in 5.46 minutes.

## page 40

### A MOTHER'S HELPING HAND

Yes. Mrs. Faulkner will have been in heaven for 2 days 16 hours and 19 minutes.

## page 42

### 3-WAY SPLIT

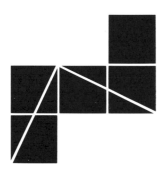

## page 42

### DEAD MAN'S SHOES

No, because they are all left shoes.

## page 43

### SANTA'S HIDDEN GIFTS

## page 44

### THE LETTER C

Here are fifty things that begin with C: cowboy; cowgirl; cravat; camera; cup; cameo; carnation; cross (crucifix); crash helmet; cat; chain; colander; crisps; clarinet; cushion; chess board; chess piece; castle; cassette; coleslaw; chair; chisel; cheese; cake; cigar; chocolates; cigarette; curlers; chin-strap; coffee; cream; cone; carrots; can; calculator; curtain; cactus; carpet; candle; clock; calender; cloud; car; cottage; church; collar; cupboard; cuff; cellophane; crayon.

## page 45

### DISPLACEMENT ACTIVITY

The boat. In the water the key displaces its volume of water; in the boat it displaces its *weight* of water. Since metal is heavier than water, the key weighs more than its equivalent volume of water.

## page 46

### DOG TOOTH CHECK

A–8; B–9; C–5; D–6; E–7; F–3; G–2; H–4; I–1.

## page 48

### THE WEEK WITH FOUR THURSDAYS

There are eleven deliberate mistakes. Woman has three legs. Soldier wearing a bra. Cow on roof. Word 'telephone' upside-down. Aeroplane has no tail wings. Door halfway up wall. Telephone box door handle on hinge side of door. Curtains on outside of building. No handle on shopping basket. Car steering wheel facing wrong way. Sitting man has no chair.

## page 49

### CHOMSKY'S DREAM

Since all Chomsky's waking beliefs are true, if he *had* been awake he couldn't have believed that he and Mimi were asleep. Therefore he was asleep. This means that his belief was false so it was not true that they were *both* asleep. Since Chomsky *was* asleep, Mimi must have been awake.

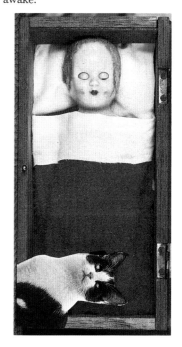

# SOLUTIONS

*page 52*

## PIEBALD SPOTTING

Neddy is horse no. 42, Norton is no. 45.

*page 54*

## TALKING SUSAN

There is no lost pound. The doll cost £25, not £27; £25 is in the shop till, £2 is in Tony's pocket, and £3 is with the uncles.

*page 56*

## ROSS SEEKS IT OUT

Ross had conclusive proof that the D'Cocos had lied when they claimed Wilson had been alone in his flat for the past half hour. When he arrived on the scene at 10.30, Ross noticed at once that the candle burning in Wilson's room was practically new and must have been lit within the past few minutes. Had it been alight since Wilson's death, it would have burned way past its 'shoulder'. In claiming that nobody had been in the room, the D'Cocos were immediately suspect. Further investigation revealed Mark D'Coco's fingerprints on the candle, clinching Ross's case.

It later transpired that D'Coco had entered Wilson's room to rifle the safe. Wilson awoke and was stabbed to death. D'Coco hit upon the idea of a bogus telephone call to throw police off the scent. But while

checking Wilson's room to see if he had left any incriminating evidence, D'Coco had lit a candle, carelessly forgetting to snuff it before leaving.

Ross's sense of smell proved too keen for D'Coco who received a twenty-five-year sentence. His wife, Ayesha, got away with a short term of imprisonment.

*page 57*

## RESTRICTED VISION

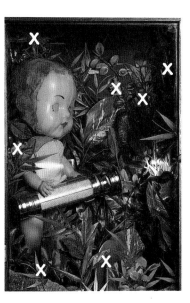

# THE END